50 True North Canadian Pies Recipes

By: Kelly Johnson

Table of Contents

- Classic Canadian Butter Tart Pie
- Maple Pecan Pie
- Wild Blueberry Pie
- Saskatoon Berry Pie
- Maple Sugar Pie
- Traditional Tourtière (Meat Pie)
- Strawberry Rhubarb Pie
- Apple Pie with Maple Crust
- Haskap Berry Pie
- Gooseberry Pie
- Raspberry Pie with Maple Whipped Cream
- Baked Beaver Tail Pie (Pastry-Inspired)
- Cranberry-Apple Pie
- Sour Cherry Pie
- Newfoundland Figgy Duff Pie
- Molasses Pie
- Pumpkin Pie with Maple Syrup
- Wild Blackberry Pie
- Pear and Maple Pie
- Butter Tart Cheesecake Pie
- Gooseberry and Rhubarb Pie
- Mixed Berry Crumble Pie
- Honeycrisp Apple Pie
- Maple-Walnut Pie
- Acadian Sugar Pie
- Peameal Bacon and Egg Breakfast Pie
- Frozen Maple Cream Pie
- Whiskey Pecan Pie
- Canadian Cheddar Apple Pie
- Blueberry Grunt Pie
- Nanaimo Bar Pie
- Canadian Prairie Saskatoon Pie
- Baked Maple Custard Pie
- Labrador Bakeapple (Cloudberry) Pie
- Peanut Butter and Maple Fudge Pie

- Caramelized Pear and Hazelnut Pie
- Wild Plum Pie
- Maple Sweet Potato Pie
- Rhubarb and Raspberry Pie
- Chokecherry Pie
- Canadian Moose Meat Pie
- Brown Sugar and Maple Pie
- Maple Cream Cheese Pie
- Grilled Peaches and Cream Pie
- Pouding Chômeur Pie
- Cranberry Orange Pie
- Hazelnut and Maple Tart Pie
- Butter Tart Ice Cream Pie
- Chocolate Maple Pie
- Newfoundland Partridgeberry Pie

Classic Canadian Butter Tart Pie

Ingredients

- 1 pie crust
- 1/2 cup butter, melted
- 1 cup brown sugar
- 1/2 cup maple syrup
- 2 eggs
- 1 tsp vanilla extract
- 1/2 cup raisins (optional)
- 1/4 tsp salt

Instructions

1. Preheat oven to 350°F (175°C).
2. In a bowl, whisk butter, brown sugar, maple syrup, eggs, vanilla, and salt.
3. Stir in raisins if using.
4. Pour into the pie crust and bake for 40-45 minutes until set.

Maple Pecan Pie

Ingredients

- 1 pie crust
- 1 cup pecans, chopped
- 3/4 cup maple syrup
- 1/2 cup brown sugar
- 3 eggs
- 1/4 cup butter, melted
- 1 tsp vanilla extract
- 1/4 tsp salt

Instructions

1. Preheat oven to 350°F (175°C).
2. Mix maple syrup, brown sugar, eggs, butter, vanilla, and salt.
3. Stir in pecans and pour into the pie crust.
4. Bake for 45-50 minutes.

Wild Blueberry Pie

Ingredients

- 1 double pie crust
- 4 cups wild blueberries
- 3/4 cup sugar
- 2 tbsp cornstarch
- 1 tbsp lemon juice
- 1/2 tsp cinnamon

Instructions

1. Preheat oven to 375°F (190°C).
2. Mix blueberries, sugar, cornstarch, lemon juice, and cinnamon.
3. Pour into pie crust and top with second crust.
4. Bake for 45-50 minutes.

Saskatoon Berry Pie

Ingredients

- 1 double pie crust
- 4 cups Saskatoon berries
- 3/4 cup sugar
- 2 tbsp cornstarch
- 1 tbsp lemon juice
- 1/2 tsp cinnamon

Instructions

1. Preheat oven to 375°F (190°C).
2. Mix berries, sugar, cornstarch, lemon juice, and cinnamon.
3. Pour into pie crust and top with second crust.
4. Bake for 40-45 minutes.

Maple Sugar Pie

Ingredients

- 1 pie crust
- 1 cup brown sugar
- 1/2 cup maple syrup
- 1/2 cup heavy cream
- 1/4 cup butter, melted
- 1 tbsp flour
- 1 tsp vanilla extract

Instructions

1. Preheat oven to 350°F (175°C).
2. Mix sugar, maple syrup, cream, butter, flour, and vanilla.
3. Pour into pie crust and bake for 35-40 minutes.

Traditional Tourtière (Meat Pie)

Ingredients

- 1 double pie crust
- 1 lb ground pork
- 1/2 cup onion, chopped
- 1/2 tsp salt
- 1/2 tsp black pepper
- 1/2 tsp cinnamon
- 1/4 tsp cloves
- 1/2 cup beef broth

Instructions

1. Preheat oven to 375°F (190°C).
2. Cook pork and onion in a skillet, then stir in seasonings and broth.
3. Pour into pie crust, cover with second crust, and seal edges.
4. Bake for 40-45 minutes.

Strawberry Rhubarb Pie

Ingredients

- 1 double pie crust
- 2 cups strawberries, sliced
- 2 cups rhubarb, chopped
- 3/4 cup sugar
- 3 tbsp cornstarch
- 1 tbsp lemon juice

Instructions

1. Preheat oven to 375°F (190°C).
2. Mix strawberries, rhubarb, sugar, cornstarch, and lemon juice.
3. Pour into pie crust and top with second crust.
4. Bake for 40-45 minutes.

Apple Pie with Maple Crust

Ingredients

- 1 double pie crust (with 2 tbsp maple syrup added to the dough)
- 4 apples, peeled and sliced
- 3/4 cup sugar
- 1 tbsp flour
- 1 tsp cinnamon
- 1 tbsp maple syrup

Instructions

1. Preheat oven to 375°F (190°C).
2. Mix apples, sugar, flour, cinnamon, and maple syrup.
3. Pour into pie crust and top with second crust.
4. Bake for 45-50 minutes.

Haskap Berry Pie

Ingredients

- 1 double pie crust
- 4 cups haskap berries
- 3/4 cup sugar
- 2 tbsp cornstarch
- 1 tbsp lemon juice
- 1/2 tsp cinnamon

Instructions

1. Preheat oven to 375°F (190°C).
2. Mix berries, sugar, cornstarch, lemon juice, and cinnamon.
3. Pour into pie crust and top with second crust.
4. Bake for 40-45 minutes.

Gooseberry Pie

Ingredients

- 1 double pie crust
- 4 cups gooseberries
- 3/4 cup sugar
- 2 tbsp cornstarch
- 1 tbsp lemon juice

Instructions

1. Preheat oven to 375°F (190°C).
2. Mix gooseberries, sugar, cornstarch, and lemon juice.
3. Pour into pie crust and top with second crust.
4. Bake for 40-45 minutes.

Raspberry Pie with Maple Whipped Cream

Ingredients

- 1 double pie crust
- 4 cups raspberries
- 3/4 cup sugar
- 2 tbsp cornstarch
- 1 tbsp lemon juice

Maple Whipped Cream

- 1 cup heavy cream
- 2 tbsp maple syrup
- 1/2 tsp vanilla extract

Instructions

1. Preheat oven to 375°F (190°C).
2. Mix raspberries, sugar, cornstarch, and lemon juice.
3. Pour into pie crust, cover with top crust, and bake for 40-45 minutes.
4. Whip cream, maple syrup, and vanilla until soft peaks form. Serve with pie.

Baked Beaver Tail Pie (Pastry-Inspired)

Ingredients

- 1 pie crust
- 1/4 cup butter, melted
- 1/4 cup brown sugar
- 1 tsp cinnamon
- 1/2 tsp nutmeg
- 1 tbsp maple syrup

Instructions

1. Preheat oven to 375°F (190°C).
2. Roll out pie crust and brush with melted butter.
3. Sprinkle with brown sugar, cinnamon, nutmeg, and drizzle with maple syrup.
4. Bake for 20-25 minutes until golden.

Cranberry-Apple Pie

Ingredients

- 1 double pie crust
- 3 apples, peeled and sliced
- 1 cup cranberries
- 3/4 cup sugar
- 1 tbsp flour
- 1/2 tsp cinnamon
- 1 tbsp lemon juice

Instructions

1. Preheat oven to 375°F (190°C).
2. Mix apples, cranberries, sugar, flour, cinnamon, and lemon juice.
3. Pour into pie crust, cover with top crust, and bake for 45-50 minutes.

Sour Cherry Pie

Ingredients

- 1 double pie crust
- 4 cups sour cherries, pitted
- 3/4 cup sugar
- 2 tbsp cornstarch
- 1 tbsp lemon juice

Instructions

1. Preheat oven to 375°F (190°C).
2. Mix cherries, sugar, cornstarch, and lemon juice.
3. Pour into pie crust, cover with top crust, and bake for 40-45 minutes.

Newfoundland Figgy Duff Pie

Ingredients

- 1 pie crust
- 1 cup dried figs, chopped
- 1/2 cup raisins
- 1/2 cup brown sugar
- 1/2 cup water
- 1/2 tsp cinnamon
- 1/2 tsp nutmeg

Instructions

1. Preheat oven to 375°F (190°C).
2. Simmer figs, raisins, brown sugar, water, cinnamon, and nutmeg for 10 minutes.
3. Pour into pie crust and bake for 30 minutes.

Molasses Pie

Ingredients

- 1 pie crust
- 1 cup molasses
- 1/2 cup brown sugar
- 1/2 cup heavy cream
- 1 tbsp butter, melted
- 1 tbsp flour
- 1/2 tsp cinnamon

Instructions

1. Preheat oven to 350°F (175°C).
2. Mix molasses, brown sugar, cream, butter, flour, and cinnamon.
3. Pour into pie crust and bake for 40-45 minutes.

Pumpkin Pie with Maple Syrup

Ingredients

- 1 pie crust
- 1 cup pumpkin purée
- 3/4 cup maple syrup
- 1/2 cup heavy cream
- 2 eggs
- 1 tsp cinnamon
- 1/2 tsp nutmeg

Instructions

1. Preheat oven to 350°F (175°C).
2. Mix pumpkin, maple syrup, cream, eggs, cinnamon, and nutmeg.
3. Pour into pie crust and bake for 50-55 minutes.

Wild Blackberry Pie

Ingredients

- 1 double pie crust
- 4 cups wild blackberries
- 3/4 cup sugar
- 2 tbsp cornstarch
- 1 tbsp lemon juice

Instructions

1. Preheat oven to 375°F (190°C).
2. Mix blackberries, sugar, cornstarch, and lemon juice.
3. Pour into pie crust, cover with top crust, and bake for 40-45 minutes.

Pear and Maple Pie

Ingredients

- 1 double pie crust
- 4 pears, peeled and sliced
- 1/2 cup maple syrup
- 1/4 cup brown sugar
- 2 tbsp cornstarch
- 1/2 tsp cinnamon

Instructions

1. Preheat oven to 375°F (190°C).
2. Mix pears, maple syrup, brown sugar, cornstarch, and cinnamon.
3. Pour into pie crust, cover with top crust, and bake for 40-45 minutes.

Butter Tart Cheesecake Pie

Ingredients

- 1 pie crust
- 8 oz cream cheese, softened
- 1/2 cup brown sugar
- 1/4 cup maple syrup
- 2 eggs
- 1 tsp vanilla extract
- 1/2 cup raisins (optional)

Instructions

1. Preheat oven to 350°F (175°C).
2. Beat cream cheese, brown sugar, maple syrup, eggs, and vanilla.
3. Stir in raisins if using and pour into pie crust.
4. Bake for 40-45 minutes until set.

Gooseberry and Rhubarb Pie

Ingredients

- 1 double pie crust
- 2 cups gooseberries
- 2 cups rhubarb, chopped
- 3/4 cup sugar
- 2 tbsp cornstarch
- 1 tbsp lemon juice

Instructions

1. Preheat oven to 375°F (190°C).
2. Mix gooseberries, rhubarb, sugar, cornstarch, and lemon juice.
3. Pour into pie crust, cover with top crust, and bake for 40-45 minutes.

Mixed Berry Crumble Pie

Ingredients

- 1 pie crust
- 2 cups mixed berries (strawberries, raspberries, blueberries)
- 3/4 cup sugar
- 2 tbsp cornstarch
- 1 tbsp lemon juice

Crumble Topping

- 1/2 cup rolled oats
- 1/4 cup flour
- 1/4 cup brown sugar
- 2 tbsp butter, melted

Instructions

1. Preheat oven to 375°F (190°C).
2. Mix berries, sugar, cornstarch, and lemon juice.
3. Pour into pie crust.
4. Mix crumble ingredients and sprinkle over the top.
5. Bake for 40-45 minutes.

Honeycrisp Apple Pie

Ingredients

- 1 double pie crust
- 4 Honeycrisp apples, peeled and sliced
- 3/4 cup sugar
- 1 tbsp flour
- 1 tsp cinnamon
- 1 tbsp lemon juice

Instructions

1. Preheat oven to 375°F (190°C).
2. Mix apples, sugar, flour, cinnamon, and lemon juice.
3. Pour into pie crust, cover with top crust, and bake for 45-50 minutes.

Maple-Walnut Pie

Ingredients

- 1 pie crust
- 3/4 cup maple syrup
- 1/2 cup brown sugar
- 3 eggs
- 1/4 cup butter, melted
- 1 tsp vanilla extract
- 1 cup walnuts, chopped

Instructions

1. Preheat oven to 350°F (175°C).
2. Mix maple syrup, brown sugar, eggs, butter, and vanilla.
3. Stir in walnuts and pour into pie crust.
4. Bake for 45-50 minutes.

Acadian Sugar Pie

Ingredients

- 1 pie crust
- 1 cup brown sugar
- 1/2 cup heavy cream
- 1/4 cup butter, melted
- 1 tbsp flour
- 1 tsp vanilla extract

Instructions

1. Preheat oven to 350°F (175°C).
2. Mix brown sugar, cream, butter, flour, and vanilla.
3. Pour into pie crust and bake for 35-40 minutes.

Peameal Bacon and Egg Breakfast Pie

Ingredients

- 1 pie crust
- 6 slices peameal bacon, cooked and chopped
- 4 eggs
- 1/2 cup milk
- 1/2 cup cheddar cheese, shredded
- 1/2 tsp salt
- 1/4 tsp black pepper

Instructions

1. Preheat oven to 375°F (190°C).
2. Whisk eggs, milk, cheese, salt, and pepper.
3. Stir in peameal bacon and pour into pie crust.
4. Bake for 30-35 minutes.

Frozen Maple Cream Pie

Ingredients

- 1 graham cracker crust
- 1 cup heavy cream
- 1/2 cup maple syrup
- 8 oz cream cheese, softened
- 1 tsp vanilla extract

Instructions

1. Beat cream cheese, maple syrup, and vanilla until smooth.
2. Whip heavy cream and fold into mixture.
3. Pour into crust and freeze for at least 4 hours.

Whiskey Pecan Pie

Ingredients

- 1 pie crust
- 3/4 cup pecans, chopped
- 3/4 cup brown sugar
- 1/2 cup maple syrup
- 1/4 cup whiskey
- 3 eggs
- 1/4 cup butter, melted
- 1 tsp vanilla extract

Instructions

1. Preheat oven to 350°F (175°C).
2. Mix brown sugar, maple syrup, whiskey, eggs, butter, and vanilla.
3. Stir in pecans and pour into pie crust.
4. Bake for 45-50 minutes.

Canadian Cheddar Apple Pie

Ingredients

- 1 double pie crust
- 4 apples, peeled and sliced
- 3/4 cup sugar
- 1 tbsp flour
- 1 tsp cinnamon
- 1 tbsp lemon juice
- 1/2 cup shredded Canadian cheddar cheese

Instructions

1. Preheat oven to 375°F (190°C).
2. Mix apples, sugar, flour, cinnamon, lemon juice, and cheddar.
3. Pour into pie crust, cover with top crust, and bake for 45-50 minutes.

Blueberry Grunt Pie

Ingredients

- 1 double pie crust
- 4 cups blueberries
- 3/4 cup sugar
- 2 tbsp cornstarch
- 1 tbsp lemon juice
- 1/2 tsp cinnamon

Instructions

1. Preheat oven to 375°F (190°C).
2. Mix blueberries, sugar, cornstarch, lemon juice, and cinnamon.
3. Pour into pie crust, cover with top crust, and bake for 40-45 minutes.

Nanaimo Bar Pie

Ingredients

- 1 graham cracker crust

Filling

- 1/2 cup butter, softened
- 2 cups powdered sugar
- 2 tbsp custard powder
- 2 tbsp milk

Chocolate Topping

- 1/2 cup dark chocolate, melted
- 1 tbsp butter

Instructions

1. Beat butter, powdered sugar, custard powder, and milk until smooth.
2. Spread into crust and chill for 30 minutes.
3. Melt chocolate and butter, then pour over the filling.
4. Chill for 1 hour before serving.

Canadian Prairie Saskatoon Pie

Ingredients

- 1 double pie crust
- 4 cups Saskatoon berries
- 3/4 cup sugar
- 2 tbsp cornstarch
- 1 tbsp lemon juice
- 1/2 tsp cinnamon

Instructions

1. Preheat oven to 375°F (190°C).
2. Mix Saskatoon berries, sugar, cornstarch, lemon juice, and cinnamon.
3. Pour into pie crust, cover with top crust, and bake for 40-45 minutes.

Baked Maple Custard Pie

Ingredients

- 1 pie crust
- 3/4 cup maple syrup
- 3 eggs
- 1 cup heavy cream
- 1 tsp vanilla extract
- 1/4 tsp salt

Instructions

1. Preheat oven to 350°F (175°C).
2. Whisk maple syrup, eggs, cream, vanilla, and salt.
3. Pour into pie crust and bake for 40-45 minutes.

Labrador Bakeapple (Cloudberry) Pie

Ingredients

- 1 double pie crust
- 4 cups bakeapples (cloudberries)
- 3/4 cup sugar
- 2 tbsp cornstarch
- 1 tbsp lemon juice

Instructions

1. Preheat oven to 375°F (190°C).
2. Mix bakeapples, sugar, cornstarch, and lemon juice.
3. Pour into pie crust, cover with top crust, and bake for 40-45 minutes.

Peanut Butter and Maple Fudge Pie

Ingredients

- 1 graham cracker crust
- 1 cup peanut butter
- 1/2 cup maple syrup
- 1/2 cup heavy cream
- 1/2 cup chocolate chips, melted

Instructions

1. Mix peanut butter, maple syrup, and heavy cream.
2. Pour into crust and drizzle with melted chocolate.
3. Chill for at least 2 hours.

Caramelized Pear and Hazelnut Pie

Ingredients

- 1 double pie crust
- 4 pears, peeled and sliced
- 1/2 cup brown sugar
- 1/2 cup chopped hazelnuts
- 2 tbsp butter
- 1/2 tsp cinnamon

Instructions

1. Preheat oven to 375°F (190°C).
2. In a pan, caramelize pears with brown sugar, butter, and cinnamon.
3. Mix in hazelnuts and pour into pie crust.
4. Cover with top crust and bake for 40-45 minutes.

Wild Plum Pie

Ingredients

- 1 double pie crust
- 4 cups wild plums, pitted and sliced
- 3/4 cup sugar
- 2 tbsp cornstarch
- 1 tbsp lemon juice

Instructions

1. Preheat oven to 375°F (190°C).
2. Mix plums, sugar, cornstarch, and lemon juice.
3. Pour into pie crust, cover with top crust, and bake for 40-45 minutes.

Maple Sweet Potato Pie

Ingredients

- 1 pie crust
- 2 cups mashed sweet potatoes
- 3/4 cup maple syrup
- 1/2 cup heavy cream
- 2 eggs
- 1 tsp cinnamon
- 1/2 tsp nutmeg

Instructions

1. Preheat oven to 350°F (175°C).
2. Mix sweet potatoes, maple syrup, cream, eggs, cinnamon, and nutmeg.
3. Pour into pie crust and bake for 50-55 minutes.

Rhubarb and Raspberry Pie

Ingredients

- 1 double pie crust
- 2 cups rhubarb, chopped
- 2 cups raspberries
- 3/4 cup sugar
- 3 tbsp cornstarch
- 1 tbsp lemon juice

Instructions

1. Preheat oven to 375°F (190°C).
2. Mix rhubarb, raspberries, sugar, cornstarch, and lemon juice.
3. Pour into pie crust, cover with top crust, and bake for 40-45 minutes.

Chokecherry Pie

Ingredients

- 1 double pie crust
- 4 cups chokecherries, pitted
- 3/4 cup sugar
- 2 tbsp cornstarch
- 1 tbsp lemon juice

Instructions

1. Preheat oven to 375°F (190°C).
2. Mix chokecherries, sugar, cornstarch, and lemon juice.
3. Pour into pie crust, cover with top crust, and bake for 40-45 minutes.

Canadian Moose Meat Pie

Ingredients

- 1 double pie crust
- 1 lb ground moose meat
- 1/2 cup onion, chopped
- 1/2 tsp salt
- 1/2 tsp black pepper
- 1/2 tsp thyme
- 1/4 tsp cinnamon
- 1/2 cup beef broth

Instructions

1. Preheat oven to 375°F (190°C).
2. Cook moose meat and onion in a skillet, then stir in seasonings and broth.
3. Pour into pie crust, cover with top crust, and bake for 40-45 minutes.

Brown Sugar and Maple Pie

Ingredients

- 1 pie crust
- 1 cup brown sugar
- 3/4 cup maple syrup
- 1/2 cup heavy cream
- 2 eggs
- 1 tbsp butter, melted
- 1 tsp vanilla extract

Instructions

1. Preheat oven to 350°F (175°C).
2. Whisk brown sugar, maple syrup, cream, eggs, butter, and vanilla.
3. Pour into pie crust and bake for 40-45 minutes.

Maple Cream Cheese Pie

Ingredients

- 1 graham cracker crust
- 8 oz cream cheese, softened
- 1/2 cup maple syrup
- 1/2 cup heavy cream
- 1 tsp vanilla extract

Instructions

1. Beat cream cheese, maple syrup, heavy cream, and vanilla until smooth.
2. Pour into crust and chill for at least 4 hours.

Grilled Peaches and Cream Pie

Ingredients

- 1 graham cracker crust
- 4 peaches, halved and grilled
- 1 cup heavy cream
- 1/4 cup powdered sugar
- 1/2 tsp vanilla extract

Instructions

1. Grill peach halves for 2 minutes per side.
2. Whip cream with powdered sugar and vanilla until soft peaks form.
3. Arrange grilled peaches in the crust and top with whipped cream.

Pouding Chômeur Pie

Ingredients

- 1 pie crust
- 3/4 cup maple syrup
- 1/2 cup heavy cream
- 1/2 cup brown sugar
- 1 cup flour
- 1/2 cup butter, softened
- 1/2 cup milk
- 1 tsp baking powder

Instructions

1. Preheat oven to 350°F (175°C).
2. In a saucepan, heat maple syrup, cream, and brown sugar until dissolved.
3. Mix flour, butter, milk, and baking powder in a bowl.
4. Pour batter into crust and drizzle maple mixture over the top.
5. Bake for 35-40 minutes.

Cranberry Orange Pie

Ingredients

- 1 double pie crust
- 3 cups cranberries
- 1/2 cup orange juice
- 3/4 cup sugar
- 2 tbsp cornstarch
- 1 tsp orange zest

Instructions

1. Preheat oven to 375°F (190°C).
2. Mix cranberries, orange juice, sugar, cornstarch, and zest.
3. Pour into pie crust, cover with top crust, and bake for 40-45 minutes.

Hazelnut and Maple Tart Pie

Ingredients

- 1 tart crust
- 1 cup hazelnuts, chopped
- 3/4 cup maple syrup
- 1/2 cup heavy cream
- 2 eggs
- 1 tbsp butter, melted

Instructions

1. Preheat oven to 350°F (175°C).
2. Whisk maple syrup, cream, eggs, and butter.
3. Stir in hazelnuts and pour into crust.
4. Bake for 40-45 minutes.

Butter Tart Ice Cream Pie

Ingredients

- 1 graham cracker crust
- 2 cups vanilla ice cream, softened
- 1/2 cup butter tart filling (brown sugar, maple syrup, butter, raisins)

Instructions

1. Stir butter tart filling into softened ice cream.
2. Pour into crust and freeze for at least 4 hours.

Chocolate Maple Pie

Ingredients

- 1 pie crust
- 1 cup dark chocolate, melted
- 3/4 cup maple syrup
- 1/2 cup heavy cream
- 2 eggs
- 1 tsp vanilla extract

Instructions

1. Preheat oven to 350°F (175°C).
2. Whisk melted chocolate, maple syrup, cream, eggs, and vanilla.
3. Pour into pie crust and bake for 40-45 minutes.

Newfoundland Partridgeberry Pie

Ingredients

- 1 double pie crust
- 4 cups partridgeberries
- 3/4 cup sugar
- 2 tbsp cornstarch
- 1 tbsp lemon juice

Instructions

1. Preheat oven to 375°F (190°C).
2. Mix partridgeberries, sugar, cornstarch, and lemon juice.
3. Pour into pie crust, cover with top crust, and bake for 40-45 minutes.

www.ingramcontent.com/pod-product-compliance
Lightning Source LLC
LaVergne TN
LVHW061956070526
838199LV00060B/4161